FREDERICK DOUGLASS

A Voice for Freedom in the 1800s

by Camilla J. Wilson

AN
APPLE
PAPERBACK

SCHOLASTIC INC.
New York Toronto London Auckland Sydney
Mexico City New Delhi Hong Kong Buenos Aires

This book is dedicated to my daughter,
Leigh Wilson-Mattson.

Cover Photo: Bettmann/CORBIS

ISBN 0-439-38082-0

12 11 10 9 8 7 6 5 4 3 2   4 5 6 7 8/0

Printed in the U.S.A.   40

First printing, October 2003

Table of Contents

Acknowledgments

I have been blessed with the support and assistance of numerous people while working on this enterprise. In particular, I would like to thank Dr. Linda Ferreira, editorial director for Scholastic, for first mentioning the project to me. I especially appreciate the efforts of Gina Shaw, my editor, for all her assistance and patience.

In addition, I would like to thank Terry Condon and George Holland for their help and hospitality in Washington, D.C., during my research there on Frederick Douglass.

I would like to thank the faculty and staff at Minnesota State University Moorhead. Dean Carol Dobitz of the College of Business and Industry has been unfailingly supportive. The Department of Mass Communications has provided me with ongoing encouragement, especially Dr. C. T. Hanson, department chair, and Marian Olson, special assistant.

Amy Phillips, Gretchen Rosenberg, Rod Miller, Kate Permenter, and Merry George have served as a much-appreciated cheering squad. My daughter, Leigh Wilson-Mattson, has been my great champion.

I thank you all.

Camilla J. Wilson
Moorhead, Minnesota
April 23, 2003

Prologue:
A Stroke of Luck

Frederick Augustus Washington Bailey knew he was lucky. True, he had been born a slave during 1817 or 1818 near Easton, a small town on Maryland's Eastern Shore. Frederick lived in a tiny wooden cabin with a dirt floor and a chimney made of clay and straw. He ate a steady diet of cornmeal mush, sometimes with a bit of pork or fish. He owned no shoes, no pants, and no jacket.

Yet, Bailey possessed one great gift for a slave child: He lived with his grandparents, Betsey and Isaac Bailey, in their own little house. He only saw his mother, Harriet Bailey, every once in a while. She would appear in the middle of the night, when she could steal away from the vast estate where she labored. Sometimes, she even managed to bring her child a treat — a ginger cake. How she acquired the cake, he never knew.

Soon after seeing her little boy, Frederick's mother would have to hurry away. It would take her the rest of the night to walk back to the slave quarters where she lived. Frederick had no father figure in his life, but he gradually learned that his father was "Old Master," Aaron Anthony, his mother's white owner.

Frederick's grandmother, Betsey, also had the reputation of being born to good luck because she had several skills valuable to her owner: She crafted extraordinary fishing nets and was well-known for being great at catching fish. She also had a way with sweet potatoes. She managed to keep her potato seedlings alive through the winter months, and then her planting talents brought her a share of the harvest. In her old age, Betsey looked after the young slave children.

Frederick's childhood took a dramatic turn when he was about seven years old. Gradually, he'd learned that something bad happened when a child reached a certain age: He or she would be sent away to work.

Frederick would work on one of his father's farms and life would be different.

The day that he was sent away began much like any other. Frederick and Betsey woke up early. It was a beautiful summer morning, and Frederick was looking forward to visiting another farm with his grandmother. The trip went on too long for his short legs, however. The plantation was twelve miles away, and Frederick became tired. By this time, Frederick was getting panicky. He realized this might be the time he had long dreaded.

"Grandmamma looked sad," he wrote as an adult. "And I could not help feeling that our being there boded no good to me."

Frederick's grandmother stood straight and strong and wore a bandanna turban over her hair. She prodded Frederick to play with the other children who were there. They were of all ages and a variety of colors, from nearly white to black. Amazingly, she singled out one boy, Perry, as Frederick's brother and two girls as his sisters, Sarah and Eliza. He knew he had a brother and sisters but he had never seen them before, and he *did* want to play. But, most of all, Frederick feared his grandmamma might leave him. Finally, Frederick followed the other children to the back of the house and stood watching, his back to the wall.

Not long after, a child ran up to deliver a cruel message to Frederick. His grandmother had left.

Frederick tore into the kitchen to see for himself: Not only was his grandmother gone, she was already out of sight. He fell to the ground and sobbed. His brother, Perry, held out some peaches and pears to comfort Frederick, but nothing would suffice. The world that Frederick had known was now totally behind him.

"[Grandmamma's] little cabin had to me the attractions of a palace . . ." he would write years later. "Its fence-railed floor — which was equally floor and bedstead — upstairs, and its clay floor downstairs, its dirt and straw chimney, and windowless sides, and that most curious piece of workmanship, the ladder stairway, and the hole so strangely dug in front of the fireplace, beneath which grandmamma placed her sweet potatoes, to keep them from frost in the winters, were full of interest to my childish imagination. The squirrels, as they skipped the fences, climbed the trees, or gathered their nuts, were an unceasing delight to me . . ."

All, all gone.

When Frederick got up from the ground, he had decided to make the best of what he had.

At the age of seven, he had already faced one of the scariest lessons of life: He would have to depend on himself.

1

Making His Way

Depending on yourself is not exactly easy when you're a seven-year-old slave child. Frederick no longer had his grandmother's baked sweet potatoes for snacks, nor a tasty tidbit of fish awaiting him at the end of a day. Instead, he, along with his brother and sisters and many other children now depended for survival on Aunt Katy, a slave woman who managed them. Aunt Katy exerted a special control on her master, Aaron Anthony, because she was a terrific cook. Yet, Frederick and many others went without even the scraps left over from food prepared for the big house that belonged to the Anthonys.

Frederick was usually hungry. Even

when he ate, it was typically bread made from coarse cornmeal and water.

In addition to hunger, Frederick needed to heal from the loss of his grandparents and his earlier way of life. Without toys or treats, entertainment or loved ones, Frederick learned to take his pleasures where he could find them.

Near the farm, Frederick saw a glorious structure: a great white windmill located on Long Point, a stretch of land that lay between the Miles and Wye rivers. He ". . . watched the winds of this wondrous mill" by the hour. The *Sally Lloyd*, a boat named after the daughter of one of the area's biggest landowners, rocked in the water close by. Next to it was a small rowboat in tow, slipping up and down in the gentle water. The road to the Lloyds' great house was paved with white pebbles from the beach.

Frederick began to daydream. He felt there must be a way out. If there were boats and beaches, there had to be other worlds beyond them as well. On the other hand, he knew he had to be careful. He learned to avoid glimmers of hope. Sometimes white boys would appear to be his friends, but eventually, they'd remember that he was a slave. He learned to pray, but realized sadly that the church was being used to justify slavery, too. There was only one thing that seemed to aid in gaining freedom: education.

By the time Frederick turned eight, two more major events took place in his life. The first involved his mother.

Captain Anthony distributed the food for all the children to Aunt Katy, who prepared and served what she wished for each child. Because she was favored by the master, she was allowed to keep her children with her, and she gave extra food to them, which meant the other children received a smaller portion. As he wrote later, Frederick often competed with Nep, the dog, for discarded morsels of food:

"Many times have I followed, with eager step, the waiting-girl when she shook the tablecloth, to get the crumbs and small bones flung out for the dogs and cats. It was a great thing to have the privilege of dipping a piece of bread into the water in which meat had been boiled, and the skin taken from the rusty bacon was a positive luxury."

In addition, Aunt Katy's usual punishment for misbehavior was to deny a child food for the day. On one particular day, Frederick had annoyed Aunt Katy and had gone all day without food.

By late evening, he was too hungry to sleep. He sat by the kitchen fire, mulling over his situation. His eyes fell on an ear of Indian corn on a high shelf. Once the others were out of sight, he slipped the ear down and shelled off a few kernels, which he roasted under the ashes in the fire. Then he retrieved the grains and stacked them on a stool. As he began to eat, his mother came in.

Frederick climbed into his mother's arms and told her how Aunt Katy had treated him. His mother tossed the corn away and instead gave him a ginger cake. She also delivered a scathing sermon to Aunt Katy.

"That night I learned as I had never learned before, that I was not only a child, but somebody's child," Frederick later wrote. "I was grander on my mother's knee than a king upon his throne."

The moment would not last long, however. Frederick's mother, Harriet, had walked twelve miles to see him, and soon she had to begin walking the twelve miles back before sunrise. It would be the last time Frederick would see his mother. She died not long after.

During that same year, when Frederick was eight, he learned something astonishing. His Aunt Jennie and his Uncle Noah had run away. This was his first notion that slaves could actually escape. Captain Anthony swore he would find them and bring them back. But the slaves eventually learned that Jennie and Noah had made it to the North. They were free!

Gradually, Frederick settled into his spot at the Anthonys'. Late in the afternoon, he drove the cows from the field up to the barn; he also tidied the yard and performed household errands. He made friends with Daniel Lloyd, the youngest son of the Lloyd family, who employed Captain Anthony. Lucretia Anthony, one of the master's grown daughters, took an interest in Frederick and occasionally gave him a slice of bread and butter if he sang as he went past her window.

Frederick especially suffered from lack of clothing. His only item of clothes was a long, rough tow-cloth shirt, which was washed once a week. At night he slept in the kitchen, either on the dirt floor or in a little closet. He had no blanket, and in cold weather he would sometimes crawl into a sack used to carry corn to the mill.

By the time Frederick was nine, Captain Anthony decided to send him to Baltimore to live with Hugh Auld, brother to Lucretia's new husband, Thomas Auld. Frederick was ecstatic. He'd heard stories about Baltimore and how slaves could travel around the city there. Some blacks were even said to be free!

Lucretia told Frederick she'd ordered him a pair of new long pants, but he couldn't have them until he scrubbed all the dirt off his body. Frederick said later that he spent the next three days in the creek.

Just as Frederick had imagined in his daydreams at the river, he sailed out on a boat. One of the ship's hands accompanied Frederick to Fell's Point, the section of Baltimore where Hugh and Sophia Auld lived. There, Frederick was "given" to the Aulds' son, Thomas. At first life seemed almost too good to be true.

Sophia Auld had never been a slaveholder before and treated Frederick more like a child than a servant. She was warm and affectionate toward him and encouraged him to hold up his head and address her directly. They called Frederick "Freddy," and he was expected to run errands, take care of Thomas, and keep the small boy safe. In return, Frederick had good, clean clothing, a decent straw bed with covers, and bread and cereal for breakfast.

Frederick received something else from one of his new owners. Sophia was very religious and read the Bible aloud to herself. Frederick decided to ask her to teach him to read. She readily agreed.

Soon, Frederick had learned the alphabet and was reading three- and four-letter words. Then Sophia bragged about Frederick's progress to her husband, Hugh. He was livid. Did she not know it was against the law to teach slaves to read?

"He should know nothing but the will of his master and know how to obey it," Auld thundered, according to Frederick. "If you teach him to read, he'll want to know how to write. . . ."

The latter was indeed true. Frederick may have been only nine, but he had fully grasped the meaning of Auld's words.

From that point on, Frederick knew he needed to educate himself.

Soon, Sophia Auld's attitude changed. Goaded on by her husband, she made every effort to keep Frederick from reading. If she found him with a book, she would grab it away. If he tarried too long someplace in the house, he might be reading and was checked up on. This only made Frederick more determined.

He always carried a copy of *Webster's Spelling Book* in his pocket when he left the house, and, if at all possible, he'd enlist the aid of the white boys he knew in the neighborhood to help him learn to read. Everywhere, Frederick looked for reading material. If he found a stray page of a book, he'd save the scrap of writing and learn to read it.

Frederick would ask the white boys many thoughtful questions. "Have I not as good a right to be free as you have?" he would often ask. Always, the boys affirmed that he did have such a right. Yet, Frederick knew that, as the boys aged, they would become like Sophia and Hugh. They would benefit too much from slavery to oppose it.

By now, Frederick could read the Bible, and yet it puzzled him how those who read the Bible did not extend its teachings to slaves.

While he was still living on his father's farm, Frederick went along to Uncle Isaac Copper's (Slaves tended to call all older males "uncle.") house to learn the Lord's Prayer. About twenty or thirty children attended the session, and Copper made ample use of hickory switches across their backs.

"Everybody in the South seemed to want the privilege of whipping somebody else," Frederick later recalled. "Uncle Isaac, though a good old man, shared the common passion of his time and country."

Frederick attempted to attend church in Baltimore. But every church he visited had a separate section for blacks. Surely, he could find a church where race did not divide people. Finally, he found the Bethel African Methodist Episcopal Church and joined.

Frederick lived with the Aulds in Baltimore for a total of seven years. Eventually, he joined Auld's shipbuilding operation, where he encountered sailors who looked on his condition as a slave with pity.

By the time Frederick was thirteen, he began looking for other books to read. He earned money shining shoes and boots whenever he was out in Baltimore. Once, he heard another boy speak of learning great speeches called "orations."

So Frederick took his entire savings — fifty cents — and purchased a popular schoolbook called *The Columbian Orator*. He memorized great speeches different people had given during the past fifty years. If learning to read had not totally ruined Frederick for slavery, learning to give speeches certainly did.

2

Back to the Fields

From the time Frederick was thirteen, his mind had become fixated on the words "I am a slave for life."

As bad as his life had been, it only got worse. His sister Sarah had been "sold south" to a Mississippi planter, which was the worst fate a slave could have. Plantations in Georgia, Alabama, Mississippi, and Louisiana were the worst in terms of the tremendous labor required to clear the land, the diseases that spread, the lack of food, and the inhumane treatment from slaveholders.

Then, when Frederick was sixteen, his situation became worse still. When Captain Aaron Anthony had died a few years earlier, Frederick had become his daughter, Lucretia

Auld's, property, but he continued to live with Hugh and Sophia Auld in Baltimore. Then both Lucretia and her brother Andrew died, and Frederick was ordered to return to the home of Lucretia's widower, Thomas Auld, who had remarried. On the ship traveling across the bay from Baltimore, Frederick resolved that, somehow, he would escape one day and be free.

From 1833 to 1838, Frederick's life moved steadily from one defeat to another. Thomas Auld and his new wife kept food under lock and key. Once again, Frederick was hungry much of the time. Occasionally, Auld's horse would come to Frederick's rescue. The horse much preferred the rich pasture at the home of Auld's new father-in-law, William Hamilton, a wealthy planter who lived about five miles away. Anytime Frederick let his owner's horse out, the horse would run off to the Hamilton's farm, and Frederick would follow to retrieve it. There, the horse was given extra food, and the Hamilton's cook would supply Frederick with bread for several days.

When Frederick had lived almost a year with Auld, who had repeatedly beaten him, Thomas attended a Methodist camp meeting. There he made a loud and fervent commitment of faith. But although prayers and hymns were heard around the house every day, the beatings did not lessen. Finally, Auld decided to send Frederick "to be broken." This meant that he would be sent to a special overseer, Edward Covey, who would break Frederick's spirit over a year's time. This would be accomplished with repeated beatings, by working him in the fields constantly, and by starving him as well.

For the first six months of that year, Frederick was beaten every week. Sometimes the welts across Frederick's back were as high as his little finger. Every day except Sunday, Frederick worked from before dawn until well after dark. During some seasons, he worked until 11 P.M. or midnight. Then an event took place that neither Frederick nor Covey ever forgot. Frederick called it "the last flogging."

Frederick was seventeen years old, more than six feet tall, and strong. However, the combination of constant overwork, lack of sleep, and hunger were taking their toll. Not only was his mind apt to be broken by Covey's daily cruelty, but his body began to suffer as well.

On Sundays, when the Coveys would set

off for church, Frederick and the other hands could rest. Frederick was so exhausted that he usually spent the day in the shade of a large tree.

Just as the sight of the windmill and the sails of the sloop had comforted Frederick when he had to come to terms with leaving his grandmother's house, the Chesapeake Bay, which was only 15 or 20 yards away comforted him in much the same way. There, ships with gleaming sails glided to and fro with crews and passengers bound for every continent on the globe. Why couldn't he go as well? The answer was always the same: He was a slave, a slave for life.

August is usually the hottest month in the South. On one day so hot that a breeze barely stirred, Frederick, along with three other hands, stood in what was called the treading yard, where grains of wheat were tramped out of the straw by horses. The men were feeding a machine that fanned the wheat when Frederick became very ill. He was extremely dizzy, and his head began to pound excruciatingly. He became so weak he could not stand up. He crawled away to a fence and was very sick.

The fan stopped turning; all four men

were needed to keep the operation moving along. Covey arrived shortly and realized something was wrong. Frederick had difficulty speaking, but when he told Covey he was sick, the overseer began to kick him. When kicks didn't work, he grabbed a hickory slab and bashed Frederick in the head.

"If you have got the headache, I'll cure you," he said, as Frederick later recounted.

In disgust, Covey left. When the headache eased, Frederick decided to go back to his owner, Thomas Auld. He could not believe that Auld would want his "property" to be treated so badly.

Frederick set out for Auld's store, a distance of about seven miles. By the time he arrived, Frederick was a sorry sight. He'd lost blood and was weak and bruised. Both his hair and his shirt were clotted with blood, he was barefoot, and his feet and legs were scarred and torn. At first, Auld seemed perturbed, but then he began to make excuses for Covey.

Finally, Auld addressed his real concern: If he took Frederick back before a year was up, he'd lose all Frederick's wages for the year. Of course, all Frederick's earnings were owned by Auld.

With a heart even heavier than before, Frederick started to trek the long miles back to Covey. Even though the upcoming events in his life were going to be decidedly unpleasant, they would have a great lifelong effect on Frederick.

On his way back to Covey's, Frederick ran into another slave he knew, a man named Sandy. Sandy had been hired out to work for another planter, but both his owner and employer treated him well. Sandy was married to a free black woman and was on his way to spend Sunday with her. He invited Frederick to spend the night at his wife's house. Exhausted, Frederick agreed.

When Frederick told Sandy about the situation with Covey, Sandy urged Frederick to fight back. He claimed to have a special root that would ward off danger. Frederick didn't really believe the root would help, but he wasn't about to turn down any good-luck charm.

When he got back to Covey's house the next day, Frederick could hardly believe his eyes and ears. Covey was on his way to church and sent him off to feed the animals. Was the root working? When Covey returned, he still showed no anger.

Covey observed his religion on Sunday, but didn't for the rest of the week. He called Frederick out before dawn on Monday and tried to grab him from behind. Frederick had rested well for a couple of days, and he remembered the words about fighting back. He knew Covey was a bully, and bullies are afraid of really fighting. Frederick managed to avoid Covey's blows. He flung Covey on the ground, holding him back far enough to keep from getting hit. Frederick was never forced to strike Covey. Covey called for his other slaves and hired hands to help him, but they all managed to avoid the fight. After two hours went by, Covey let go of Frederick and announced as if he'd won, "Now, you scoundrel, go to your work. I would not have whipped you so hard if you had not resisted."

For the remaining six months that Frederick stayed with Covey, he was never beaten again. Because Covey knew what was in store for him if he attacked Frederick, from that point on, he only made threats.

By early 1836, Frederick was on his way to a new temporary master's house. He was William Freeland, and he worked an "old, worn-out farm," as Frederick described it.

But Freeland was decent for a slave owner; "[Freeland was] the best master I ever had until I became my own master," Frederick later said.

Frederick was still a field slave, which he preferred to be rather than a house slave. In the house, the work was usually a bit easier, but slaves had to constantly deal with the moods and whims of owners, along with whatever work had to be done. It was easy to become attached to a white owner, who could make fateful, life-changing decisions regarding a slave. Sometimes slaves might be rented out to other owners, as had happened to Frederick. Slaves might also be sold or have their child or spouse sold and sent away forever. In the field, owners were mainly interested in how much work they could get out of slaves.

At the Freeland plantation, Frederick had enough to eat and was well-treated. He was seldom in the fields at night or before daybreak. It did not take long for his mind to turn to bettering his life and that of his friends.

There were four other field slaves who worked with Frederick: two brothers, Henry and John Harris, along with Handy Caldwell and Sandy Jenkins, the man who had befriended Frederick earlier and given him advice about Covey. Henry and John Harris were Freeland slaves and had grown up on the plantation.

Frederick soon began to tell others about education and the advantages of being able to read and write. He began a Sunday school for the other workers, and, before long, twenty or thirty men would gather every week for their lessons from *American Spelling Book*. They all managed to find spellers because youngsters often threw them away after learning to read. During the summer, they met under trees. During the winter, a free black man allowed the group to meet in his house, which was considered dangerous because it was still illegal for slaves to learn to read and write.

Learning to think means not only learning to read and write, it also means learning to question, and slave owners were certainly right in assuming that slaves who learned to think would begin to question their fate. Before long, Frederick and a few of the group began to talk about escape.

It was early spring of 1836, and Frederick was now nineteen. Along with teaching other slaves to read, he discussed ideas with them. He would also talk about things he'd read and learned from *The Columbian Orator* and about the possibility of escape. The slaves decided among themselves that April would be a good time to try to escape.

The group began to plan. It included Henry and John Harris, Sandy Jenkins, and two other men. They were in a difficult location as the area around Easton, Maryland, is surrounded by water on three sides. The land to the north not only included slave owners and sheriffs, but also traders and kidnappers who might hunt down escaping slaves and resell them in the South. But the group finally decided on an escape plan. They would take a boat from a nearby slaveholder, William Hamilton, and would set off across the Chesapeake Bay on a 70-mile boat trip. They would use the North Star to guide them to freedom. With the plan in place, Frederick carefully wrote out passes for each member of the group.

Each pass had a version of the following letter:

"This is to certify that I, the undersigned, have given the bearer, my
servant John, full liberty to go to Baltimore to spend the Easter holidays."

Each was signed, via Frederick, with a slave
owner's name.

Misgivings plagued the men, especially
Sandy Jenkins, who was married to a free
black woman. A few days before they were to
escape, Jenkins had a series of dreams. He
interpreted them as warnings.

On the morning they were set to leave,
they went to the fields very early. When the
horn sounded for breakfast, they returned to
the house just as a group of constables arrived with two slaves bound together. The
word was out.

Frederick said later in life that he suspected Freeland might easily have picked up
on the idea that they were plotting escape.
They were too cheerful and were singing
hymns much too joyfully, especially "O Canaan, sweet Canaan, I am bound for the land
of Canaan."

The group was rounded up but did not include Sandy, who somehow was not found
out. Later, the group wondered if he had re-

ported them, but they liked him too much to believe that.

Frederick and John Harris had been in the kitchen when the constables arrived. When Henry came in from the barn, the policemen tried to grab him. Henry resisted and ran around the kitchen, refusing to have his hands tied.

Frederick managed to toss his pass into a fire during the fray. Luckily, Betsey Freeland, William Freeland's wife, came into the area with a plate of biscuits and handed them out. But she was furious at Frederick, who was suspected of writing the passes for the group. He was assumed guilty because he was the only one of the group who could write.

"Eat [your pass] with your biscuit," Frederick told the others as they set out, walking to the jail.

"We were literally dragged, that morning, behind horses, a distance of fifteen miles, and placed in the Easton jail," Frederick later wrote.

All denied they were plotting escape. Slave traders flocked to the jail, assuming they would all be sold. Soon after Easter was over, William Freeland and William Hamilton arrived at the jail to pick up their slaves. While Freeland believed the men were innocent, Hamilton felt otherwise. He was not only certain there was a plot, he blamed it all on Frederick.

About a week later, Thomas Auld arrived to pick up Frederick. Frederick eventually learned that Hamilton had informed Auld he had to send Frederick away or he would shoot him. So after a few days at home, Auld informed Frederick he was being sent back to Baltimore to live with Thomas's brother, Hugh, again. He would go back to work in the shipyards. Once again, Frederick had been very lucky. He had planned to escape, been found out, and was sent back to Baltimore, the city from which he'd always believed he could make the easiest possible escape.

MRS. AULD TEACHING HIM TO READ.

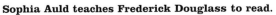

Sophia Auld teaches Frederick Douglass to read.

Frederick Do

DEVOTED TO THE RIGHTS OF ALL MANKIND, W

VOL. X.---NO. 48.   ROCHESTER, N. Y.

FREDERICK DOUGLASS' PAPER.

IS PUBLISHED EVERY FRIDAY MORNING,
At No. 25, Buffalo Street, (opposite the
Arcade,) Rochester N. Y.

TERMS OF SUBSCRIPTION.

Single copies, one year (invariably in advance,)
$1 50; five copies and over $5 00.

POSTAGE.—Inside of Monroe County, free; to
any part of New York State payable in advance,
3 cts. to any part of the United States, 6 cts. per
quarter.

Selected.

THE EXILED NEGROES OF CANADA.

Report of The Tribune's Special Commissioner.

I.

THE NEGROES OF TORONTO.

The neighboring British provinces have long
been the refuge of the fugitive slave, and every
increase on this side of the border of the ri-
gor of the laws to ensure his return to his master causes him to look with more eager long-
ing to a country in which his liberty is secure
and he possesses the same political rights as
the rest of mankind. There the law is a pro-
tector, and the public, always more rigidly
virtuous when the crime to be condemned is
that of a neighbor, will see that it is neither
violated nor evaded. The desire of safety and
of political equality, valued the more highly
from its being strenuously denied, has attracted
numbers of colored men, both fugitive slaves
and free, to a climate naturally uncongenial to
them. What has been the effects of this
security and this political equality upon them?
Have they improved morally and socially?—
Have they become more industrious and more
intelligent, or, in the absence of all restraint,
have they become idler and more vicious?—
Are they capable, under favorable circumstan-
ces, of becoming good citizens in a well ordered community, or is there a want in their or-
ganization which renders the overseer and the
taskmaster necessary to their well-being? A
hurried trip through a portion of Upper Canada, undertaken as a relaxation from profess-
ional toil and care, has enabled the writer to
answer some of these questions, at least to his
own satisfaction. He claims no peculiar fit-
ness for his task beyond an honnest desire to
learn the truth, to see facts as they exist, un-
colored as far as possible by prejudice or theo-
ry; and if, with every well-wisher of his

open piano stood on one side of the room, a
melodeon occupied the pier between the win-
dows; on the walls hung a well-painted por-
trait of the owner of the house, and engrav-
ings representing the Queen, her husband and
children. Though early in September, the
evening being somewhat cool, a small woodfire
blazed upon the hearth. Our host was a light-
colored mulatto of middle age, short, spare,
well and strongly built, with a large square head
and a firm, sagacious looking countenace.—
Many years previous he had emigrated, with
his wife and elder children, from Mobile, bring-
ing some capital with him. He was by trade
a carpenter, and industry, economy and judi-
cious investments had gradually raised him to
his present position. His wife, apparently in
ill health, was darker than himself; the children,
somewhat darker, too, than the father, consis-
ted of a well-built lad of 19, a slender girl of
17 and a boy of 12, who was busy at the table
writing a school exercise. The elder boy was
studying medicine, and, at the same time pre-
paring himself to pass the classical examination,
which, in Upper Canada, is a necessary preliminary to taking the degree of Doctor of
Medicine, and had advanced so far as to read
Cicero De Senectute. The language of the
young people was correct and well chosen, and
both in manner and conversation they would
be looked upon as good examples of the
youth of the middle class of any nation. In
the course of the evening the young man
played several pieces on the piano, and he
and his sister sang duets with skill and
taste.

The physician, Dr. A. T. A., is a mulatto, a
native of Virginia, but for a long time resident
in Philadelphia. Finding that he was unable
to obtain access to the medical schools in that
city, he came to Toronto and entered there
upon the study of medicine, attending the lectures of the faculty of medicine of Trinity College. He has not yet obtained a degree, since
though he passed a creditable examination in
medicine, he failed in the classical examination,
which is a necessary preliminary to graduation.
He is now prepared for this ordeal, and, after
being examined again upon the prescribed
books of Plato and Cicero, and translating
the necessary amount of good English into
bad Latin, will become an M. D. He, however, is already engaged in practice, and has
received the appointment of Physician to the
Poor-house, which, as it is in the gift of medical men, is a proof of the advancement he has
made. He both talks and writes well, and is
generally respected throughout the city.

The livery-stable keeper is a fine example,

Of these, 78 only were coloured—not 1½
cent. Now, as the coloured people consti-
at the lowest computation, between two
three per cent. of the total population of
ronto, this is a high and, I may add, an u
pected evidence of the general good con
of the coloured people; and the value of
increased when we remember that they all
iginally belonged to the class in which c
against order and property are the most
Of the whole number of persons arrested. 4
were males and 1,051, or nearly one-fo
were females; while of the colored peopl
were males and 8 only, not quite one-o
were females.

The printed report of Mr. Sherwood re
as was stated, to the total number of arr
Of those, 1,922 were summarily punished
fine. In 273 cases the charges were withdr
and 230 cases were dismissed. Thinking
possibly the actual commitments to jail m
set a different face upon the matter, we
tained from Mr. George L. Allan, the int
gent keeper of the jail at Toronto, the mo
ly return of commitments to that prison 1
October 1, 1855, to July 31, 1857, a peri
twenty-two months, transcribing them f
the books of the jail in his presence.
total commitments amounted in that per
to 3.370, of whom 62, not quite two per c
were coloured. Immediately after the pas
of our Fugitive Slave law, Mr. Allan infor
us that there was a sudden increase in the n
ber of commitments among the coloured p
ple, almost wholly for petty larcenies. Thi
crease of crime Mr. A. attributed to the n
ber of fugitives who flocked into Canada w
out any means of support and whom des
tion drove to theft; in a few months, as
new-comers found employment, this incr
disappeared. On the whole, Mr. Allan
decided, in the opinion that, as regards cr
against the law, the condition of the colo
people was better than that of the mass of
population.

II.

THE NEGROES OF HAMILTON A
CHATHAM.

At Hamilton, in a population of 24,
there are from 400 to 600 colored peo
among them blacksmiths, carpenters, pla
ers and one wheelwright. There are
churches, small frame buildings, a Baptist
a Methodist, but they are not well suppor
and neither of them at present has a reg
resident clergyman. Many of the colored
are reputed to possess property, but I do

le outward appearance of wealth. For the
time in my travels the women were with-
hoops, and some strapping lassies I met,
ered with huge flat Bloomer hats, their nat-
lly broad shoulders rendered broader by a
e , their clinging skirts, innocent of starch,
ss or whalebone, presented to one fresh from
city a sight sufficiently strange. Here at
was an inversion of the common order of
ags! The principal hotel at which we put
was a large, wooden barrack of a building,
entrance on a level with the unpaved
et, and sharing necessarily somewhat its
or and appearance. Inside, things were
re inviting ; the rooms were clean, neat
comfortable, and the beds, except that
y were stuffed with feathers, irreproachable.
found the landlord, a huge, jolly English-
n, at the head of his own tea-table, carving
ound of beef big enough to have fed the
mmon Council of a city ; and, for the first
e since we had been in Canada, in a place
arming with negroes, the waiters at table
re white, and females. The town consists
one long street—King street—closely
lt, in which the stores are all situated, while
dwellings, mostly surrounded by gardens,
scattered over streets crossing and run-
parallel to it.

Despite its unpromising appearance, Chatham
ms an active and stirring place. In the
vn there are three saw-mills, two shingle-
ls, two potash factories, two sash and blind
tories, four flour-mills, four brick-yards, sev-
l iron-founderies, three or four wagon fac-
ies, three cabinet warehouses, three brewer-
and two distilleries. It is a port of entry,
exports a large amount of lumber, staves,
agles, bricks, drain tiles and flour. A large
amboat was, when we were there, being
ded for Buffalo, and two smaller steamers
a brig were lying in the stream. Before
present depression in business, which pre-
s equally in Canada as in the United States,
en steamboats and a dozen sailing vessels
re been seen in the port at one time, com-
tely filling up the river.

Of this busy town about one-third of the
pulation are colored people, and they ap-
to contribute their full quota towards its
ustry. Among them are one gunsmith, four
binet-makers working on their own account
d employing others, six master carpenters, a
mber of plasterers, three printers, two watch-
kers, two ship-carpenters, two millers, four
ster shoemakers, six grocers, and a cigar-
ker. Unskilled workmen find abundant em-
yment in the various mills, in agricultural

tion and culture than among the same class at
Toronto.

In Kent, the County in which Chatham is
situated, many of the coloured people are ag-
riculturists, residing upon and cultivating their
own farms. Many of them are represented as
doing exceedingly well. One farm, owned and
occupied by a coloured man recently deceased,
and still cultivated by his family, was generally
allowed by those not disposed to favor the
blacks, as well as by their well-wishers, to be
the model farm of the neigh d. Some,
without capital or skill, and probably; too,
without sustained industry, do not succeed ;
but it is generally admitted that, on the whole
they make better farmers than the Irish, and
far better than the French Canadians, a considerable number of whom reside in the immediate neighborhood of Chatham.

From the Liberator.

**Memorial of the Colored Citizens of Wis-
consin :**

*To the Honorable, the Legislature of the
State of Wisconsin.*

We, the undersigned, colored inhabitants of
the State of Wisconsin, would once more exercise the *right,* which is guaranteed to *all
the people,* peaceably to assemble, and petition
the Government for a redress of Grievances.
We complain of Art. 3d, Sec. 1st of the Constitution of the State of Wisconsin. We now
ask your honorable body to regard our feeble
request, and remove this *heel of oppression*
and disability which rests upon us, as contain-
ed in the Article and section referred to, and
thereby gives us an opportunity to become respected citizens of the State. We
complain of that part of the Section which
disallows to us the right of franchise and at
the same time grants it to others who immigrate
from foreign lands, and who do not understand
the Constitution, Government and Laws as
well as ourselves. We do not say, neither do
we *believe,* that men of foreign birth, immigra-
ting to this asylum of the oppressed, should be
deprived of any of the rights and blessings
which this government has confirmed upon
them ; but we *do* say, that the same rights
and blessings should be extended to us. In
addition to all this, is it not proper to submit
to your honorable body to say if it be right
justice, or *common sense,* that we should be
subject to taxation without representation ?
We are informed—by those who claim to
know—that a vote was taken by the people in
1849, and that a majority of votes were cast
in favor of suffrage—thereby taking away
We would ask your honor-

siderable section of it. At all events, Kansas
is at this moment suffering in many other par-
ticulars under the incubus of Border-Ruffian
legislation, from which her people are entitled
to be relieved at the earliest possible moment.
—[*New York Tribune.*

SLAVERY IN THE STATE OF NEW YORK.

Through the Lemmon case, just argued in
our First Judicial District, the "National Democracy" has delivered its Laws and its Poli-
tics respecting Slavery in the State of New
York. In the lengthy argument of Charles
O'Conor, pleading for Virginia and for the
right of property in man, the following points
were deliberately taken, and boldly maintained The free men of New York can see the
condition to which "Democracy" is determined to bring the Empire State :

"The ancient general or common law of
this State authorized the holding of negroes
as slaves therein. The Judiciary never had
any constitutional power to annul, repeal, or
set aside, this law.

"The Judiciary never had any power to
annul, repeal, or set aside, the slave law of
this State, which we have shown existed with
the sanction of the Legislature prior to the
Revolution.

"The Judicial department has no right to
declare Negro Slavery to be contrary to the
law of nature, or immortal, or unjust, or to
take any measure, or to introduce any policy,
for the suppression of it, founded on any such
ideas.

"It cannot be pretended that there ever was
in England, or that there now is in any State
of the Union, a law, by any name, thus out-
lawing slavery. The common law of all these
countries has always regarded it as a basis of
individual rights.

"In fact there is no violation of the princi-
ples of enlightened justice, nor any departure
from the dictates of pure benevolence, in holding negroes in a state of slavery.

"Negroes, alone and aided by the guard-
ianship of another race, cannot sustain a civ-
ilized social state.

"Who shall deny the claim of the intellectual white race to its compensation for the
mental toil of governing and guiding the negro
laborer ?

"It follows, that in order to obtain the measure of reasonable personal enjoyment, and
of usefulness to himself and others, for which
he is adapted by nature, the negro

Frederick Douglass was the first African American to own a newspaper. He
first published *The North Star* on December 3, 1847, in Rochester, New York.
Later, he changed the title to *Frederick Douglass' Paper.*

Frederick Douglass's first book, published in May of 1845. The book cost fifty cents and became a best-seller in the United States and abroad.

FREDERICK DOUGLASS' OLD OFFICE

This view of the office where *The North Star* was printed has been reproduced from a pen-and-ink drawing of a woodcut used by the *Rochester Union and Advertiser*, March 2, 1895.

Frederick Douglass's first office, in Rochester, New York, where his newspaper was printed.

**Underground Railroad Pass written by
Frederick Douglass. It reads:**

My Dear Mrs. Post:

**Please shelter this sister from the house of bondage
till five o'clock — this afternoon — she will
then be sent on to the land of freedom.**

**Yours Truly —
Fred. K.**

Douglass and his grandson

**Frederick Douglass's house as it stands today.
The house was made a National Historic Site in 1988.**

3

Escape to the North

Frederick returned to Baltimore in 1836 ". . . the very place, of all the others, where I most desired to live," he later wrote. Yet, as many before and after him have found, going back to a place where you've once lived is never the same: Something will have changed.

Times were harder. Hugh no longer had his own shipbuilding business. Now he worked as a foreman, a supervisor in charge of groups of other men. Tommy was a teenager, and ". . . the time had come when his friend must be his slave" as Frederick observed. This was extremely painful for Frederick, who had loved Tommy dearly. Frederick didn't stay in the household long, however, as Hugh Auld soon hired him out to a major shipbuilder named William Gardiner.

During the earlier years when Frederick had worked in shipbuilding, he'd learned about caulking, the practice of making the bottoms of ships airtight by applying a waterproof paste, and driving the sections of the ship together snugly. Once he joined Gardiner's operation, he was expected to train as a caulker's apprentice. This was an excellent skill to master, but there was a major risk, too. Most of the caulkers were white men who desperately needed the wages they earned. Now those earnings would be severely undercut if slaves performed the same task.

Rather than taking the direction of an overseer or a foreman, Frederick now had to answer to any of eighty-odd carpenters who were busy building two large ships for the Mexican government. No one had any time to teach an apprentice, yet all the carpenters yelled out orders.

When Frederick had worked in a shipyard before, whites and blacks had worked together. Shortly before Frederick arrived in Baltimore, however, the white workers had notified the shipyard owners that they didn't want to work with free blacks. Frederick was not free, but that didn't stop the workers from being angry; having a slave work meant that he was doing a white worker's job for much lower wages. Tensions festered for about eight months.

Then, one day a white carpenter changed his taunts to a physical attack. Frederick hit back, grabbing the man and dumping him against the dock. One-on-one, Frederick could hold his own. But bullies often like to team up.

Four of the other caulkers came after Frederick, some armed with bricks. At least fifty men watched as the four pummeled Frederick, one using a brick and another a handspike. Finally, one severely kicked Frederick in the left eye. His eye gushed blood, and Frederick thought he'd lost the use of it.

When he finally escaped, Frederick went home to the Aulds. Hugh Auld behaved in the opposite way from his brother, Thomas — he was furious at Frederick's attackers. His wife, Sophia, washed the blood away from Frederick's face and began to cry when she saw his wounds. After they had patched him up, Hugh took him to see a magistrate, a lower-level judge who could file charges against the attackers. The judge refused to consider the case: He had to have white witnesses.

Frederick's appearance — battered and bruised with an eye almost gouged out — didn't matter to the judge. He would do nothing. The word of a black person counted for nothing in Maryland. None of the fifty or so white workers who witnessed the assault would testify to what had really happened.

Disgusted with the state of justice in Maryland, Auld took Frederick back home to recover. Sophia continued to dress Frederick's wounds and, fortunately, his eye was saved.

Once his health improved, Auld decided to hire Frederick out at the shipyard where he worked as foreman. Frederick's apprenticeship as a caulker continued and, within a year, he was able reach the highest salary scale paid to apprentice caulkers who had reached the highest level of training.

As soon as matters had eased a bit for Frederick, he began to think more about freedom and how he could attain it. He knew if he tried to escape again, he would have to succeed. With his previous escape attempt still hanging over his head, Frederick knew if he was caught he'd be sold south for sure. So, Frederick began to plan carefully.

Soon he hit upon a new idea — hiring himself out each week to an employer. He thought he could also manage to hide some money for his escape fund. Hugh Auld considered the proposition to let Frederick hire himself out. Then he came up with a formula that he thought would entice Frederick to work harder but would actually return all the money back to himself.

Frederick could hire himself out, but every week, regardless of the amount of work earned, he had to pay Auld three dollars plus another three dollars for room and board, as well as paying for all his clothing and caulking tools. Frederick agreed. This was a hard bargain because work varied from week to week, clothing wore out quickly, and theft and loss of tools were common. Nonetheless, Frederick persevered, and every now and then he managed to save a quarter or a dollar for his fund.

Since he was now able to travel around Baltimore, Frederick slowly added bits and pieces to his education. He made friends with people who had picked up elements of the education Frederick lacked, including literature, geography, and mathematics.

Because Frederick was still enslaved, he was prohibited from joining any of the forty or so benevolent societies maintained by free blacks in the city. However, due to the debating skills he'd acquired from his old favorite book, *The Columbian Orator*, he was finally allowed to join the East Baltimore Improvement Society. He frequently took part in debates held by the society, an activity that polished the skills he would need later in life. He also met a young, free black woman named Anna Murray. Eventually, they began to plot Frederick's escape from the city. She had nine years of savings to contribute to the attempt.

It was 1838, and Frederick was twenty-one. By now, just as events in his life seemed to be moving toward fleeing, Frederick made a mistake.

As long as he paid Auld on time according to the agreement, all was well. Usually, Frederick paid Auld after work on Saturday night. But one day Frederick agreed to go with some friends to a religious meeting outside Baltimore. He worked late and then had to decide either to go home to pay Auld or leave with his friends. Thinking he could pay Auld the next day, Frederick went with his friends. Once there, he ended up staying an extra day.

When he returned to Baltimore, he immediately went to pay Auld, who was livid with anger. Frederick was a slave. Had he forgotten? He had to ask Auld's permission before leaving town, before taking any action. Auld ordered him home and commanded him to bring his tools back. From now on, Auld would make the payment arrangements.

Typically, Frederick would still have gone out looking for work, but he decided to stay home all week, much like a sulking child with a parent. At the end of the week, Auld was furious. Frederick finally realized this was not a course that would bring him freedom, so he set out to find work and returned with a good caulking project. Auld was satisfied, and Frederick realized he'd better attempt his escape before he made another major mistake.

It would be forty years before Frederick fully revealed the methods he used to escape from Baltimore. He didn't want to give any aid to slaveholders attempting to thwart escapees, nor did he wish to enable the slave traders and kidnappers to catch runaways. There were even blacks — both free and enslaved — who would report slaves on the run. Frederick also had to be sure that no one known to whites had assisted him. Anyone who helped a slave escape could face the full wrath of the law.

There were free black sailors in Baltimore, which was a port that bordered the North as well as the South. Such sailors had to always carry what was termed "protection," or papers that described the sailor's height, weight, and coloring, and indicated the person was free. Such papers had to be renewed frequently for a fee, which was very difficult for free blacks.

Finding a sailor friend who was especially tall was difficult, but Frederick finally found someone who fit his description except for his coloring. The paper carried an eagle as a designation of approval. This was going to be the best opportunity Frederick would have for a long time, so he seized it and assumed a different identity.

Going north from Maryland overland was quite dangerous and would take considerable time. The area near the Maryland–Pennsylvania border was home to many kidnappers who were on the lookout for runaways. So Frederick decided to make a bold move: He would escape as if he were a free man. He would go north by train and boat. He started out on a Monday, as if he were working, as usual, on a caulking job.

Knowing that his coloring would likely tip off a train conductor if his papers were carefully examined, Frederick decided to jump aboard the final car of a train headed to Philadelphia. A friend pitched his bundle of belongings on board. He was off!

When the conductor came along, there were many passengers to check in the Negro car and Frederick needed to purchase a ticket. He supplied his document and quickly engaged the conductor in conversation. He knew if the conductor had time to think about his coloring, the game would be over. The train man did ask for his "free papers," but Frederick had an answer. He never took them on a train trip — they were too valuable. He only took his sailing papers on a journey, his "only pass was the American Eagle."

The conductor nodded and hurried on, and Frederick momentarily felt safe. That didn't last long, however. As he sat in a station where a southbound train was also stopped, he recognized a white slaveholder he knew well. Luckily, the man did not recognize Frederick in his sailor's uniform, and the train pulled away without incident. Later on, he encountered a German blacksmith for whom he had once worked. The white man looked at him closely, Frederick later said, but said nothing. Because he was foreign-born, Frederick thought the man knew who he was but decided to let him go.

At the Pennsylvania border, Frederick took a steamboat to Philadelphia. Onboard was a black deckhand, a man he had known in Baltimore. The worker kept asking Frederick questions. Where was he going? When would he be going back? Finally, Frederick escaped to a different section of the boat until they docked in Philadelphia. From there he took a boat to New York City. The trip from Baltimore had taken only twenty-four hours. He was free!

It was September 4, 1838. He was on free soil in New York City. But it didn't take long for Frederick to find out that he was not quite as free or as safe as he thought.

Amazingly, not long after he arrived in

New York, by chance he met a man that he knew. William Dixon, as the man was known in New York, had been "Allender's Jake" in slavery. Dixon had been owned by a doctor whose son had shown up in New York City and had almost recaptured him. Looking around for observers, Dixon warned Frederick about New York.

The streets were unsafe according to Dixon, who reported that many Southerners came to the city, along with kidnappers seeking runaways. He cautioned that Frederick had to be especially careful of blacks, for many would be tempted by the few dollars they could earn for informing on a slave.

The worst thing Frederick could do would be to head for the wharves — the most likely place for a skilled caulker to go — or to boardinghouses operated for blacks. Officially, New York might be free territory, but it was segregated. Those were the first places Auld and slave traders would look for him, and soon posters with his description would be put up. Dixon was even afraid to spend too much time talking to Frederick — he thought that maybe Frederick would betray him. Soon Dixon, carrying a whitewash brush that he used in his work, vanished down an alley.

This was horrible news. The first thing Frederick meant to do was find the wharves and secure a job. He only had a little money left, and he knew no one in New York. That night, he slept among the barrels piled on a wharf.

Eventually, Frederick approached a sailor by the name of Stuart, who actually took him home for the night. The next day, Stuart took Frederick to see David Ruggles, an officer on the Underground Railroad. Ruggles hid Frederick for a few days, and he sent his papers back home to Baltimore to the sailor who'd lent them to him. Frederick also sent for Anna Murray, who immediately set off for New York. When she arrived, they went to see a prominent Presbyterian minister, the Rev. J.W.C. Pennington. They had no money to pay the fee for the marriage, but on September 15, 1838, Pennington performed the ceremony and wished them well.

Once Ruggles learned that Frederick was a caulker, he decided that the best place for Frederick and Anna to go would be New Bedford, Massachusetts. They would be much safer there, where many ships for the whaling industry were being built and fitted out.

So, two days after Frederick and Anna were married, they said their good-byes to Ruggles and set out for the wharf. Frederick carried three important items in his pocket that day: his marriage license; a five dollar bill from Ruggles (his wedding gift), and the name of a contact in Newport, Rhode Island.

They put their few belongings aboard the *John W. Richmond*, a steamship that plied the route between New York and Newport, Rhode Island, a city near New Bedford. During the trip, however, Frederick and his wife could not enter the ship's cabin. Regardless of the weather — hot or stormy or cold — they had to stay on deck. They did so gladly: They were free, they were married, and a wonderful world of freedom lay ahead.

4

Free in
Massachusetts

Once Frederick and Anna arrived in Newport they faced a new dilemma: They lacked enough money for the final segment of their journey, the relatively short trip from Newport to New Bedford. The yellow letters NEW BEDFORD beckoned on the stagecoach that had stopped along the wharf where the young couple stood. They paused, uncertain what to do next.

However, as fortune would have it, two Quakers stood nearby waiting for the same stagecoach. One of the men realized Frederick's hesitation and spoke to him: "Thee get in."

And so they did, boarding the stage but still not knowing how they would pay when they arrived. They had no money to buy food along the way, but when they got to New Bedford, the driver agreed to hold on to their belongings, including several music books, until Frederick returned with their fares.

The couple had the names of a Mr. and Mrs. Nathan Johnson, part of the Underground Railroad connections that assisted former slaves as they made their way to the North. The Johnsons were retired and extended every kindness to Frederick and Anna. They fed them and put them up in their home and promptly lent them the two dollars needed to pay their fares and retrieve their baggage.

The Johnsons also taught them about New Bedford. They assured Frederick that he need not fear recapture. However, the first order of business was to change Frederick's last name. Thomas and Hugh Auld and the slave catchers would be seeking Frederick Bailey. Nathan Johnson had recently read a book titled *Lady of the Lake*, so he suggested Frederick become Frederick Douglass, taking the name of one of the Scottish characters. Therefore, Frederick Douglass had his beginnings in New Bedford, a city that granted him freedom but denied him many of its benefits. Yes, a black person could be free in New Bedford, but at a price. There was a different evil to deal with — racism. Nonetheless, Massachusetts still offered Frederick a way of life he'd only dreamed about.

Everything in the South conspired to keep slaves ignorant about everything but the tiny little world in which they worked — the plantation system and its immediate community. Every aspect of life on a plantation and in the surrounding world was set up to reinforce the economic system of slavery. No one questioned the way things operated, and very little information passed back and forth about life in other states, much less other countries. The churches, businesses, and the political and social structures all supported slavery. And, most of all, lack of education closed all avenues to advancement. New Bedford was indeed a new world and, in many ways, Frederick Douglass was a new man.

While looking for work in New Bedford, Frederick spotted a sizable load of coal that had been dumped outside the home of a Unitarian minister. Douglass went to the kitchen door and asked if he could move the coal inside.

"What will you charge?" the minister's wife asked, according to an account Douglass later gave.

"I will leave that to you," he replied.

When he finished, she handed him two silver half-dollars.

"I clasped this money realizing that I had no master who could take it from me — that it was mine — that my hands were my own," he recounted.

Soon, Douglass began to seek out work as a caulker. He had spent years in apprenticeship, and New Bedford was well-known for its shipbuilding, especially whaling ships. Douglass learned of a well-to-do antislavery man named Rodney French, who was readying a ship for a whaling trip. French hired Douglass as a caulker, a job that paid two dollars per day. However, when he went down to the ship, he was informed that every white worker would automatically leave if he began to caulk. So Douglass instead found work as a common day laborer, a job that only paid one dollar per day. Douglass was indeed free in the North, but his job and his pay still hinged on the color of his skin.

For the next several years, Douglass took whatever work he could find. Sometimes he blew the bellows at a brass factory, a job that involved opening and closing a large device to drive air into the works. This was hot work over a furnace, a hard, manual-labor job that was later done by a steam engine. Sometimes he loaded and unloaded ships at the docks, scrubbed cabins on ships, sawed wood, or shoveled coal. Anna Douglass worked hard as well.

She was a household worker in the city and did laundry at home after work. They had a daughter, Rosetta, born in 1839, and a son, Lewis Henry, born the year after that. Anna Douglass had brought with her from Baltimore a trunk containing bed linens and pillows, dishes, and knives, forks, and spoons. These special possessions made their two rooms a home.

They marveled at comparisons of life in Baltimore and New Bedford. In Baltimore, everything was done by manual labor, usually slave labor. In New Bedford, wells and pumps supplied water and reduced carrying. Oxen were used to load and unload on the docks.

"In a southern port, twenty or thirty hands would be employed to do what five or six men, with the help of one ox, would do at the wharf in New Bedford," Douglass later wrote. There were also sinks and drains, washing machines, and wringing machines.

Both black and white children went to school together in New Bedford, but as adults they did not attend lectures together. This was a sore disappointment to Douglass, who was always looking to increase his education. Eventually, however, he would learn about a group of people who called themselves abolitionists and were determined to have slavery abolished in the United States. Everyone — white or black — could attend the abolitionists' lectures.

Not long after reaching New Bedford, a young man stopped Douglass and asked if he wanted to subscribe to *The Liberator*, a newspaper published by William Lloyd Garrison, a famous antislavery spokesman. Douglass said he had no money and had just escaped from slavery, but the young man willingly took him on as a subscriber. In 1839, Douglass began hearing abolitionists like Garrison and Wendell Phillips speak at local lectures.

"Prejudice against color is rebellion against God," Garrison thundered.

"Every week *The Liberator* came," Douglass wrote. "And every week I made myself master of its contents."

Douglass already knew the worst of slavery and racism. Now he was beginning to form the philosophy that would occupy him for the rest of his life.

5

Abolition:
The New Religion

It was 1841. Douglass had heard abolitionists speak on various occasions and
had continued to read every issue of *The Liberator*. Garrison's written words in the paper
excited Douglass: Here was a white man who
was devoting his life to abolishing slavery.

Then Frederick found out that Garrison
would speak in New Bedford. He attended
the meeting held in early August of 1841. He
was enthralled by the effect Garrison had
on his audience. Douglass now knew what
he had to do: He would make antislavery
speeches the same as Garrison did. Then, in
August, something extraordinary happened:
Garrison was present when Douglass spoke
at a New Bedford antislavery meeting.

Garrison took note of Douglass. It was unusual to have a former slave addressing a group. It was difficult to even imagine this man as having been a former slave. He was well-educated and spoke eloquently, as if he had been trained in public speaking. But most important, his words carried great emotional appeal with his audience.

The abolitionists were having a hard time getting their voices heard. The southern planters and the other people who supported slavery had rallied their supporters and were fighting abolition. The pro-slavery groups argued that God himself ordained, or approved of, slavery. They quoted the Bible, and ministers preached that slavery was the only way to control Africans. They also reasoned that slaves were much better off than factory workers in the North, because slaveholders took excellent care of their slaves from birth to death. They said the old plantation was a warm home for life.

The abolitionists were looking for a way to respond to the pro-slavery proclamations. *The Liberator* ran a letter to Garrison in January of 1842, stating that "The public have itching ears to hear a colored man speak, and particularly a slave. . . . Multitudes will flock to hear one of this class speak," the letter continued, adding that it would "be a good policy to employ a number of colored agents, if suitable ones can be found."

Garrison was already looking for former slaves who could add his or her personal experiences to the antislavery crusade. Douglass had no way of knowing that attending an antislavery convention in Nantucket, Massachusetts, would put him in contact with Garrison, the white man he most admired. The result of this trip would alter the course of the rest of Douglass's life.

Garrison was white, but he shared a background with Douglass of extreme poverty. He had little formal education, and had been farmed out to various tradesmen as a child laborer. Garrison's experiences presented another world to Douglass, a world in which a white child had also struggled and suffered.

In the South, whites had generally been divided into three groups: planters; whites who benefited from slavery; and poor whites, who had no land and hardly any more rights than slaves. In the North, there were far more groups of people, with many more divisions in the middle class. There were also sizable immigrant groups.

Garrison's background was Irish and

English. Garrison's mother, Fanny Lloyd, had become such a devout Baptist in her youth and so disturbed her father with her evangelism that he sent her to live with an uncle. While there, she met her husband, a swashbuckling sailor named Abijah Garrison.

The two were married, setting in motion a series of events that brought hardship to both of them and their children. They settled in Newburyport, Massachusetts, a seaport where the ships often traveled to the West Indies. Soon, Garrison's father displayed more interest in rum, a liquor from the West Indies, than in religion or his family. After an evening when Fanny broke all her husband's rum bottles, Abijah abandoned them all.

Fanny, as religious as ever, worked at any job she could find to care for her children. Women were barred from almost all positions except housework and nursing. Garrison was devoted to his mother and, as a child of five, did his share by peddling molasses candy on nearby street corners. The young Garrison often played at other people's houses and frequently took any food scraps home with him. Eventually, Fanny had to leave the children with friends so she could work as a nurse and a household worker to pay for their keep.

Then Fanny was offered what appeared to be a good job in Baltimore, so she moved her family there. In that city, Garrison saw the effects of slavery at every turn. He accumulated little education and had to make up for it later, like Douglass, when he was an adult. Garrison hated his life in Baltimore and longed to return to Newburyport. When he was eleven, Fanny sent him back to apprentice with a cabinetmaker, but he ran away. Soon, Fanny was able to apprentice her son to a printer, the editor of the local newspaper, *The Newburyport Herald*. This event turned out to be as significant to Garrison as Douglass's experience in purchasing and learning to read *The Columbian Orator*. For the next seven years of his apprenticeship, Garrison did not return to Baltimore.

All of Fanny's heavy work exhausted her, and she eventually became ill with fever and tuberculosis. She sent for Garrison. He managed to spend several months with his mother before she died. Fanny was not happy about Garrison's desire to be a writer.

In the last letter he received before reaching Baltimore, his mother wrote, "You have no doubt read of the fate of such characters, that they generally starve to death in some garret or place that no one inhabits; so you may see what fortune and luck belong to you if you are of that class of people."

Significantly, not only would he achieve fame and a certain amount of comfort in his field, but at his mother's bedside he encountered the subject of much of his later work: slavery. His mother was being lovingly cared for by a slave woman. Garrison had never ceased to worship his mother, and he transferred those feelings to the cause of ridding the world of slavery. Together, Garrison and Douglass would carry the movement far.

After Garrison's apprenticeship was over, he moved from one printing position to another until he, too, found his two callings: abolition and his own newspaper, *The Liberator*.

When Frederick Douglass traveled to an abolitionist meeting in Nantucket in August of 1841, a celebrated group of antislavery speakers were slated to speak. William Lloyd Garrison was there, along with Wendell Phillips and other prominent speakers. One of the group, William C. Coffin, had heard Douglass speak in New Bedford, and invited him to speak.

"I trembled in every limb," Douglass would later write. "This is about the only part of my performance that I distinctly remember."

However, once Douglass began to recount his experiences as a slave, the audience became excited. Afterward, the only thing people would remember, according to accounts, were Douglass's words. Thereafter, Garrison made Douglass his topic, and, together, the two speakers were breathtaking.

For Douglass, the door to fame and fortune had just opened wide. At the end of that first meeting, the general agent of the Massachusetts Anti-Slavery Society pleaded with Douglass to become a lecturer for the group. Douglass finally agreed to take the position for three months. He decided to move his family to Lynn, Massachusetts, in the fall of 1841. Speaking out against slavery would certainly reinforce what Douglass already knew: He might not face slavery in the North, but he encountered racism everywhere. He delivered a speech in Lynn, a two-pronged attack on both slavery in the South versus racism in the North.

For the next several months, Douglass traveled all over the North with several white abolitionists; they lectured at meetings held in city after city.

While religion in the South had failed Douglass, serving only to prop up slavery, he exulted in a new kind of religion — abolition. "My whole heart went with the holy cause. . . ." he wrote. "In this enthusiastic spirit I dropped into the ranks of freedom's friends and went forth to the battle. For a time I was made to forget that my skin was dark and my hair crisped."

Douglass traveled in eastern Massachusetts speaking and gathering subscriptions to *The Liberator*. While he was glorying in the wonderful reception to his speeches, he began to encounter a different type of reaction from other former slaves. Any black who admitted being a runaway might indeed be kidnapped, but within the black community, admitting to being a former slave was considered degrading. Slaves had certainly not asked to be slaves, yet some people looked down on blacks who admitted they had once been slaves. Douglass had no time for this! He paid no attention.

In January of 1842, Douglass became a full-time, permanent lecturer on antislavery. He was careful not to admit who his owner was or where he lived. In the early months, the other speakers kept Douglass speaking about his own experiences, rather than commenting on them or calling for actions to abolish slavery. They thought a former slave wouldn't be the right speaker for such weighty subjects. Soon Douglass resisted and began to speak out fully.

More and more, people began to doubt that Douglass had ever been a slave. How was it possible? He didn't look the way people thought a slave should look. He didn't sound like a slave was expected to sound. He was highly skilled at oratory and reasoning and argument.

"[T]hey believed I had never been south of Mason and Dixon's Line" [which determined slaveholding areas], he wrote.

Again and again, northerners repeated, "He's never been a slave, I'll warrant you."

So, Douglass moved to the next step, following the lead of Garrison. He decided to write a book. He continued to speak, sometimes going as far west as Indiana and Ohio.

And, despite the fact that northern states were free, whites still exhibited racism and enforced segregation.

For black travelers, segregation was not only demeaning, it was exhausting and sometimes even life-threatening. The railroads, steamboats, and hotels all practiced segregation. Arrangements for places to stay had to be worked out before trips, and last-minute arrangements could leave African Americans without a place to sleep, forcing them to stay outside in rain, snow, or ice.

When Douglass traveled by steamship, he did not resent the whites who went into their cabins to sleep. Still, he held a special place in his heart for those who would brave the weather with him. He especially appreciated Wendell Phillips, James Monroe, and William White, and wrote of Monroe: "I have known James Monroe to pull his coat about him and crawl upon the cotton bales between decks and pass the night with me, without a murmur."

Trains could be even more difficult. They typically bought first-class tickets, but once a conductor caught sight of Douglass's skin, he would usually decree that he must sit in what was termed the "Jim Crow" car, the one for passengers with colored skin. The Jim Crow car was usually dirty, cold, and old. Sometimes the conductor would call for reinforcements, and Douglass might wind up being beaten. More than once, he held on to his seat in the first-class coach until he was finally evicted.

Officials on the railroad that ran through Lynn, Massachusetts, where Douglass and his family now lived, finally decided to avoid stopping at his town. A number of townspeople did business in Boston, so this created a problem.

The superintendent of the railroad was Stephen A. Chase. Douglass wrote of him, "With an air of triumph he told us that we ought not to expect a railroad company to be better than the evangelical church, and that until the churches abolished the Negro pew we ought not to expect the railroad to abolish the Negro car."

One of Douglass's friends dryly noted that the railroad often allowed monkeys and dogs in first class, and churches did not.

During 1843, the crowds for meetings continued to grow. Douglass and other speakers addressed thousands of people in Clinton County, Ohio, a wonderful event that was soon to be eclipsed by their experiences in Indiana.

In Richmond, Indiana, the speakers were pelted with rotten eggs. In Pendleton, Indiana, when they were attending a meeting of Quakers, about sixty ruffians appeared, tore down the platform, and attacked the speakers. One man lost several teeth, another was knocked down, and Douglass was beaten into unconsciousness by the mob. Probably assuming that he was dead, the group, whom Douglass termed "mobocrats," mounted their horses and took off. A local Quaker took Frederick home to recover. His hand was broken in many places and never fully healed.

The antislavery speakers included many men who would have a profound effect on the nation. Not only were there speakers like Garrison and Wendell Phillips, but there were young men who would go on to become famous as diplomats, congressmen, and journalists.

Finally, during the winter of 1844–1845, Douglass finished his first book, *Narrative of the Life of Frederick Douglass*. William Lloyd

Garrison and Wendell Phillips, two of the most famous men in the country, wrote introductions, and the book appeared in May of 1845. Sold for fifty cents, the book became a best-seller in the United States and sold widely internationally. Over the next three years, the book had more than nine editions in England alone.

Now the world knew who Frederick Douglass really was. He was Frederick Bailey, who had belonged to Thomas Auld of Easton, Maryland. Now there was no denying that Douglass really was an escaped slave, no doubt that he knew firsthand of what he spoke. But the glee of the slave traders and the slave kidnappers and those — both white and black — who resented his success, was profound. Douglass's friends were unanimous in one respect: There was no state or territory in the United States that could be counted on to protect Douglass. He would have to flee the United States — immediately.

6

Fleeing to England

Fleeing the country was a difficult decision for Douglass. He and his wife now had four children, and being an antislavery lecturer was not a high-paying job. Yet, if he were recaptured and sent back to Baltimore to work, or, more likely, sent to be a field hand in the South, everyone in the family would suffer. His *Narrative* came out on May 28, 1845, to much acclaim. Yet appearing in public — even in Boston and northern New York state — made his capture all the more likely. Douglass had been thinking of taking his antislavery message to Great Britain. The time had come to book passage. But, of course, it would not be easy.

James N. Buffum, a friend from Lynn and a member of the antislavery movement, chose to go along with Douglass. Buffum attempted to purchase first-class tickets to Liverpool on the *Cambria*, a steamer that was part of the Cunard Line. Douglass was unable to get a cabin on the ship. For what the ticket seller called "complexional" issues, referring to the color of Douglass's skin, he had to travel in steerage, the least expensive section of the ship. Steerage was below the other decks and was where immigrants usually stayed.

"The insult was keenly felt by my white friends, but to me such insults were so frequent and expected that it was of no great consequence whether I went in the cabin or in steerage," Douglass later wrote.

Douglass may have dismissed the matter of his accommodations, but he did not hesitate to spread his antislavery message. He carried many copies of the *Narrative* along with him for passengers to purchase, and he was eager to talk with passengers about slavery. During the day, Douglass promptly left steerage and went upstairs to the promenade, the upper deck where passengers could walk back and forth. He sold copies of his book and visited with other passengers. There were southerners onboard who detested the presence of an African American. Near the end of the journey, Douglass was almost thrown overboard.

Many of the passengers wanted Douglass to speak about slavery and his experiences as a slave, and the ship's captain agreed. The night before they reached Liverpool, Douglass gave his antislavery lecture. Several young men from New Orleans and Georgia began to shout out disapprovingly, saying his statements were lies. Douglass then began to read some of the laws that applied to slaves. The pro-slavery group of men rushed at Douglass, fists flying. The captain knocked one man down and summoned his crew members.

"I'll put you in irons," the captain reportedly told the group. They slunk away, fearful of winding up in shackles.

Once they landed, the group tried to get even with Douglass. The southerners reported to the press about Douglass, denouncing him and charging him with being a "worthless and insolent Negro." Strangely, this turned out to be the best kind of advertising for Douglass.

"They unintentionally did me the kindness of winning me an immediate audience in Great Britain," Douglass wrote. The

British welcomed Douglass and his anti-slavery message. While in Liverpool, he arranged to have another 2,000 copies of the *Narrative* printed, which he would be able to distribute.

From Liverpool, Douglass traveled to Ireland, where he spoke in Dublin, Cork, and Belfast. As Martin Luther King, Jr. would do in the next century, Douglass refused to limit his message to only one area of injustice; he spoke against the oppression of the Irish by the British. He also spoke out on temperance, the movement to ban alcohol. The abuse of alcohol was creating enormous upheaval in families.

"I cannot allow myself to be insensible to the wrongs and sufferings of any part of the great family of man," he wrote. "I am not only an American slave, but a man and, as such, am bound to use my powers for the welfare of the whole human brotherhood."

Douglass spent four months in Ireland. It was the first time he had ever lived free from racism. From Ireland, Douglass made his way to England and Scotland.

In October of 1845, Douglass received word that Thomas Auld, his slave master, had sold him to his brother, Hugh. Word circulated that Hugh Auld had stated that he was going to see that Douglass was captured and shipped south. This was certainly no time to return home.

Eventually, he joined William Lloyd Garrison in England during the summer of 1846, and the two of them spoke throughout England. In November, Garrison sailed for the United States. Abolitionists in England offered to give Douglass a permanent home there and began to raise money to bring his family over as well. This would have given him the opportunity to live his life free from slavery and racism.

Douglass thought long and hard about this offer. On the one hand, it was almost an offer of paradise to one who was still considered a slave. On the other, such a move might be wonderful for him and his family, but would do nothing to free slaves still in bondage. So Douglass declined.

Back in Lynn, Massachusetts, his wife, Anna, struggled to feed her four small children. She no longer had Douglass's lecture fees from speaking in the United States. She sent her daughter Rosetta to live with Lucretia Mott in New York. She was barely surviving, working as a shoe binder in Lynn.

Sometimes she did laundry for other families as well. She had never had any formal education and could hardly write, yet she still managed to support antislavery meetings.

After the abolitionist press began to write of threats to Douglass's freedom by Hugh Auld, said to be planning to capture Douglass "cost what it may," antislavery groups in England began to raise money to purchase his freedom papers.

Finally, in October 1846, they raised $711.66 and paid Hugh Auld for Douglass's freedom. On December 12, 1846, he became a free man when legal papers of manumission — documents granting him his independence — were filed in Baltimore.

Amazingly, there were antislavery groups in the United States who opposed the purchase of his freedom. They charged that the British antislavery groups were dabbling in the "right to traffic in human beings." They wrote editorials and spoke out in meetings.

Yet, in England, Douglass was not only famous but beloved. More than 1,400 people gathered to render him a public farewell. He told the group that he had learned "what it was for the first time in my life to enjoy freedom."

When he reached Liverpool and boarded the ship for his voyage back to the United States, he encountered the same prejudice he had faced on his trip to England the year before. The Cunard agent forced him to give up the cabin he had booked, saying he had created a commotion on his prior trip and that they were taking precautions.

Douglass wanted to return home, so he agreed. But, like the southerners had done on his arrival, he wrote a letter to *The London Times*, saying he was sure the public would not approve of the action.

British editorialists were horrified. "England Made Ashamed," said one. "Disgraceful Prejudice Against a Man of Color," said another.

Douglass's friends and admirers indeed prevailed.

S. Cunard, head of the Cunard line, wrote *The Times* that ". . . nothing of the kind will ever take place in the steamships with which I am connected."

This brought Douglass great satisfaction, yet there were many more steamships and trains and buses to be boarded during his lifetime. But Douglass was going home — and he was going home a free man.

7

The Civil War

When Frederick Douglass left the United States for England in 1846, he was a runaway slave who had made a name for himself with abolitionist groups, particularly in the North. When he returned eighteen months later, he was world famous, the author of a book that had become a best-seller in English-speaking countries. He was well-known on both sides of the Atlantic for his eloquent speeches on a variety of issues — not just slavery — but also on world peace, Ireland's freedom from England, and as a voice for the poor. His friends in England, unable to keep him there permanently, had seeded his next major venture: a newspaper.

This venture demanded a new location,

Douglass decided, so he moved his family to Rochester, New York, a city long known as a haven for fugitive slaves and intellectual thought. Rochester was also a significant stop on the Underground Railroad, which had helped Douglass escape slavery nearly ten years earlier.

Matters were even worse for escaped slaves. In 1850, the southern states managed to get the Fugitive Slave Act passed in the U.S. Congress. Now the penalty for aiding slaves would be prison. This generated even more drastic action on the part of many who supported freeing the slaves, including insurrection — fighting back violently against slavery. The country was very close to a civil war between the slave states and the free states. In some cases, family members fought family members over the issue, and racial groups fought among themselves as well.

When Douglass returned to the United States from England, he brought with him approximately $2,500 raised by his English friends to start a newspaper. He traveled to Boston and consulted his old friends in the antislavery groups. They were appalled at the idea of his starting a newspaper, and argued he knew nothing about editing one.

There were already two major antislavery newspapers. William Lloyd Garrison's *The Liberator* and the *Anti-slavery Standard*. His friends didn't see why there should be another. Douglass pointed out that there had never been an African-American newspaper and that he had the money to begin one. His friends still disagreed, but Douglass did not lose heart. He might not know anything about writing and editing a newspaper, and he might not know anyone in Rochester, but he did know that Rochester was a city that might support his work.

The North Star appeared for the first time on December 3, 1847, carrying editorials signed by Douglass. The newspaper came out every week "at a cost of $80 per week," Douglass wrote, with a subscriber list of 3,000. Eventually, Douglass had to mortgage his house to provide funds for the newspaper. Friends then came to his aid to help him increase the number of subscriptions and save his house from creditors. He also changed the name of the newspaper to *Frederick Douglass' Paper*, a title that ensured people knew who had started the publication.

For the next decade, Douglass's life was one of constant speaking and publishing. In

1855, he published a second autobiography, *My Bondage and My Freedom*.

Some of Douglass's most important work during this period, however, was done via the Underground Railroad. The Fugitive Slave Act made it impossible for slaves to just make it to the North — they had to go all the way to Canada to escape the clutches of southern slaveholders. Rochester was a port city on Lake Ontario, so slaves could take boats across the lake to Canada, or they could cross the Canadian border near Niagara Falls. Because of Douglass's connections with antislavery groups, he was able to help hundreds of escapees.

During this period, Douglass met John Brown, a man who believed in violently overthrowing slavery. Douglass met Brown in Springfield, Massachusetts, in 1847. They had discussions throughout the next few years, and in February of 1858, Brown stayed at Douglass's home in Rochester while developing plans for a slave revolt. At that time, Brown secreted some papers in Douglass's desk.

In August of 1859, Douglass met Brown at a stone quarry near Chambersburg, Pennsylvania. There, Douglass learned that Brown planned to attack slaveholders at Harper's Ferry, West Virginia. Douglass decided not to participate. Douglass believed an assault would be viewed as an attack on the government, not on slavery.

During October, Douglass was speaking in Philadelphia when he learned that Brown along with a group of men had started their revolt. Brown's band of twenty-one men included five blacks. They invaded Harper's Ferry, carrying considerable arms and ammunition for the slaves. Brown's group quickly captured most of the whites, killed three men, and declared the slaves free. Next, they took control of a rifle factory and an arsenal where ammunition was kept. This was the greatest fear of slaveholding whites: The slaves would violently revolt. Virginia and West Virginia authorities acted decisively.

Lieutenant Colonel Robert E. Lee, who would later become commander in chief of the Confederate military and naval forces of Virginia, sent out a group of U.S. troops and overpowered Brown and his group. Brown was captured.

The soldiers found letters from abolitionists, along with other documents, in Brown's belongings. Soon a telegram arrived in Philadelphia, saying that these abolitionists, including Douglass, were to be arrested. Fortunately, Douglass knew the telegraph operator, who came to warn him. Douglass asked some of his friends to go with him to a ferry that would take him to New York. One by one, his friends decided they needed to go in other directions — they were all scared to be seen with Douglass. Only one friend, Frank Turner, accompanied Douglass to the ferry. Reaching New York was just the first step. Douglass realized he needed to leave the country. Knowing he might be arrested for possibly helping Brown, Douglass set out for Canada.

By then, Douglass remembered the papers Brown had left in his desk in Rochester. He sent a message back to the telegraph operator in Rochester, telling him to contact his son and have him destroy documents left in his desk. This included a constitution Brown had written. Brown believed his men would benefit from guidelines of government even while they hid out in mountain retreats during a revolt.

Douglass heard rumors of attempts to arrest him in Rochester as he desperately made his escape to Canada. In early November of 1859, Douglass boarded a steamer leaving from Quebec, going by way of the north passage to England. The trip was cold and miserable; before they left Labrador, temperatures dropped to four degrees below zero.

When Douglass arrived in England, he was immediately in demand for speaking appearances. The British knew all about John Brown's slave revolt. Brown and all but five of the group had been captured or killed. Brown had been hanged and his cohorts executed. In the North, Brown had become a hero and a song, "John Brown's Body," extolled his life and beliefs. The search for other conspirators continued for a time in the United States, so Douglass stayed in England and France for six months. Then tragedy struck the Douglass household.

In March of 1860, Douglass received word that his ten-year-old daughter, Annie, had died. She was "the light and life of my house," he later wrote. Heartbroken, he returned home. Interest in seeking out others who might have known of Brown's intent was fading. There was a much bigger national crisis at hand. The candidates for the 1860 presidential election were campaigning, and there were fears that the results of the election might spark the southern states to secede, or leave the Union.

Three major political parties dominated the election. Stephen A. Douglas represented the western Democrats, split into two groups by slavery; Douglas believed that the people in a territory should decide whether or not to allow slavery. John C. Breckenridge represented the southern Democrats, who said that any slaveholder should be able to take his slaves into any territory and hold them there, regardless of what others believed. Abraham Lincoln was the candidate for the Republicans; Lincoln believed that the U.S. government should decide whether slavery would exist in a territory. Lincoln also believed that slavery should be kept within the slave states and eventually abolished. Frederick Douglass and the abolitionists backed Lincoln.

Abraham Lincoln won by an extremely narrow margin, and the southern states began to carry out their threats of secession. For the next few months, the North tried to please the South by coming up with ways to keep the Union together, regardless of the cost to slaves. One after another, however, southern states began to secede. It was not until the attack on Fort Sumter, the tiny federal fortress on an island off the coast of South Carolina, that the North rose up to defend itself. April of 1861 was a momentous month: The Civil War had begun.

Douglass immediately saw that the result of the war would be the end of slavery or the end of the Union. He began a campaign to include black troops in the Union Army. This was not popular in the North, not even with Lincoln.

The Lincoln administration informed the South that slavery would still exist. Northern generals told slaves that there would be serious consequences if they tried to escape to gain their freedom.

"This faith [in the abolition of slavery] was many times shaken by passing events," Douglass wrote, "but never destroyed."

Southern troops used slave labor not only in the fields but also to build forts and dig trenches. Battle after battle took place before the North began to see that including blacks in the armed forces was useful. Unfortunately, at first, the North only allowed blacks to serve as labor, not as soldiers. They frequently sent blacks to places prone to yellow fever.

"I was convinced that it was to the colored man's advantage to get an eagle on his button, a musket on his shoulder, and the star-spangled banner over his head if he could possibly do so," Douglass wrote.

The war was not going well for the North in 1863. Lincoln's advisers convinced him that freeing the slaves would change the direction of the war. If the South had to cope with freed slaves, the North would win. So Lincoln issued his Emancipation Proclamation, which only freed slaves in the slave-holding states. Douglass went to speak to President Lincoln and stated the case for treating black soldiers equally with whites. It didn't happen, but Massachusetts did raise the first black regiment in the Civil War, and three of Douglass's sons joined.

Federal troops controlled Baltimore, and, in November of 1864, Douglass returned to Baltimore for the first time since leaving twenty-six years before. He spoke six times there and met his sister Eliza, whom he had not seen in thirty years.

Douglass supported Lincoln's reelection bid in 1864 and attended his inauguration, the formal ceremony that opened Lincoln's second term as president. Douglass also attended the inauguration ball and was greeted there by Lincoln.

The president spent little time in office, however. He was assassinated in April of 1865. Although Douglass might have attended the inauguration ball, the New York Common Council would not allow any blacks to participate in the funeral procession when Lincoln's body passed through the city. Eventually, Lincoln's widow, Mary Todd Lincoln, learned about this episode and sent Douglass Lincoln's walking stick.

The end of the Civil War brought Douglass a personal gift: He met his brother Perry for the first time in forty years and helped him bring his family to Rochester.

The Civil War had cost the country greatly, and many soldiers and civilians lost their lives. Much of the South lay in ruins. The slaves were officially free, but a lot of work remained to be done. Racism and segregation were still practiced in both the North and the South.

Frederick Douglass had become the most prominent black man in the United States. Soon it would be time to go to Washington, D.C.

8

The Fifteenth Amendment

There was enormous hope for the rights of blacks after the Civil War. However, as would happen time and again in United States history when there was a great public push for equality, a massive backlash followed.

After Lincoln was killed, Andrew Johnson became president. He was from Tennessee and did not move quickly to establish the political rights of blacks. Douglass began to campaign for black suffrage — the right to vote — throughout the country. He also supported women's rights, including suffrage for all black and white women, who had never been allowed to vote in the United States. Eventually, his leadership in multiple issues would lead to public office.

The end of the Civil War and freedom for American blacks at first created a crisis for Douglass. He had spent decades publishing antislavery newspapers and speaking out against slaveholders. Now blacks were free! What was he to do now?

Eventually, he began to receive requests to speak before groups throughout the United States, and not just on racial topics. He began to give speeches at graduation ceremonies at colleges. And he began to speak for ratification of the Fifteenth Amendment to the U.S. Constitution.

There were various groups meeting around the country on extending voting rights to black men and all women. The groups did not always get along. Douglass had a long history of supporting voting rights for women and for black men. In 1848, he had been the only man to attend the first Women's Rights Convention at Seneca Falls, New York. Famous black abolitionists like Sojourner Truth supported Elizabeth Cady Stanton and Susan B. Anthony in their efforts to gain the right to vote. After the Civil War, white men began to concur that black men should vote, but they still felt women should not. This was infuriating to black and white women, yet most black men, including Douglass, believed they should accept the amendment. Thus, the Fifteenth Amendment passed in 1870, and women—black and white—were denied the vote for another fifty years, until 1920.

In 1872, Douglass's Rochester home was destroyed by fire. Many believed that arson was involved. His family was safe, but Douglass lost much of his writing. Ironically, Harvard College had recently asked him to donate his papers to the school, but he had not made up his mind. Now they were gone.

Yet, Douglass took action, much as he did after he was caught trying to escape in Maryland. He promptly decided to go in another direction. He moved his family to Washington, D.C. Eventually, he headed the Freedmen's Bank and, in 1877, President Rutherford B. Hayes appointed him as U.S. Marshal for the District of Columbia.

During the same year, Douglass decided to take a trip back to eastern Maryland, where he grew up. He addressed a group of blacks and whites there and also visited his old master, Thomas Auld, shortly before Auld died.

In 1878, the Douglasses purchased Cedar Hill, a twenty-room estate in Anacostia, an area outside Washington, D.C. They bought the house in spite of a "covenant" in the neighborhood. Communities in the North often excluded groups of people by covenants, or agreements that new owners signed when they purchased houses. Sometimes blacks, Jews, Catholics, and other groups were barred from buying houses. This tactic would be used by southerners for a hundred more years, until segregation was finally outlawed. Many subdivisions were built that included covenants.

In 1881, Douglass published his third autobiography, the *Life and Times of Frederick Douglass*. The book did not sell well. However, he received a presidential appointment to become Recorder of Deeds for the District of Columbia. In August of 1882, his wife, Anna, died. Throughout the nearly forty-four years they were married, she had supported his efforts and sometimes provided all the monetary support for herself and their children.

According to Rosetta Douglass Sprague, one of the Douglasses' daughters, the great deeds of Frederick Douglass were "a story made possible by the unswerving loyalty of Anna Murray."

In 1884, Douglass remarried. He married Helen Pitts, his former secretary, who was twenty years younger than he. She was also white, which created an uproar in his family, as well as among people who did not believe that different races should marry.

By the mid-1890s, Douglass, unfortunately, had a new horror to speak against: lynching. Whites in both the North and the South were lynching blacks, using vigilante groups to whip them and terrify blacks to "keep them in their place," and sometimes kill them if they did not comply.

On February 20, 1895, Douglass attended the morning session of the National Council of Women in Washington. Later that day, he had a heart attack and died at Cedar Hill. He would not live to see women get the right to vote, which would take another twenty-five years. He did not live to see students of all races admitted to all public schools, which would not happen for another fifty-nine years, after the *Brown* v. *Topeka* Supreme Court decision in 1954. It would take another civil rights movement, fueled by the public speeches of another man, Martin Luther King, Jr., to result in landmark changes for blacks. But Frederick Douglass was the voice for change in the 1800s. He led the way on the path to freedom.

Epilogue: The African-American Voice of the 1880s

After the death of Frederick Douglass, the family held funeral services at Cedar Hill. His body lay in state at the Metropolitan African Methodist Church in Washington, D.C., and people came to mourn from far and wide. No one had done more to speak out against slavery and racism in the 1800s than Frederick Augustus Washington Bailey Douglass.

Douglass understood the price and the rewards of taking a stand.

"If there is no struggle, there is no progress," he said. "Those who . . . favor freedom and yet [belittle] agitating are men who want crops without planting the ground, they want rain without thunder and lightning. They want the ocean without the awful roar of its many waters."

Many throughout the past two centuries have read Douglass's words, calling for changes to right wrongs. He planted the seeds, which have resulted in the achievement of many of the greatest changes in our nation's history. But the struggle — and the progress — continue.

Sources

Bode, Carl. *Maryland*. New York: W. W. Norton & Company, Inc., 1978.

Cornelius, Janet Duitsman. *Slave Missions and the Black Church in the Antebellum South*. Columbia: South Carolina Press, 1999.

Diedrich, Maria. *Love Across Color Lines*. New York: Hill and Wang, 1999.

Douglass, Frederick. *The Frederick Douglass Papers*. John W. Blassingame, ed. New Haven: Yale University Press, 1979.

Douglass, Frederick. *Life and Times of Frederick Douglass*. New York: The Crowell-Collier Publishing Company, 1962.

Encyclopedia of Afro-American Culture and History. Jack Salzman, David Lionel Smith, Cornel West, eds. Vol. 2. New York: Simon & Schuster and Prentice Hall, 1996.

Foner, Philip S. *The Life and Writings of Frederick Douglass*. 4 vols. New York: International Publishers, 1950.

Goldin, Claudia Dale. *Urban Slavery in the American South 1820–1860*. Chicago: The University of Chicago Press, 1976.

Hare, Lloyd C.M. *Lucretia Mott*. New York: Negro Universities Press, 1970.

McDaniel, George W. *Hearth and Home: Preserving a People's Culture*. Philadelphia: Temple University Press, 1982.

Merrill, Walter M. *Against Wind and Tide*. Cambridge: Harvard University Press, 1963.

The African-American Encyclopedia. Michael W. Williams, ed. New York: Marshall Cavendish, 2001.

Thomas, John L. *The Liberator: William Lloyd Garrison*. Boston: Little, Brown and Company, 1963.

Yee, Shirley J. *Black Women Abolitionists*. Knoxville: The University of Tennessee Press, 1992.

About the Author

CAMILLA J. WILSON teaches journalism at Minnesota State University Moorhead. She has written for newspapers and magazines for more than twenty-five years. She has spent considerable time in Asia, where she has written about social and political issues from China to Bangladesh. She spent more than two years in Vietnam during the war there and wrote for a group of small newspapers. She has written *Rosa Parks: From the Back of the Bus to the Front of a Movement*, and *George Washington Carver: The Genius Behind the Peanut*, also published by Scholastic Inc.